THE PACIFIC OCEAN

A TRUE **BOOK**

by

David Petersen and Christine Petersen

Children's Press®

A Division of Scholastic Inc.

New York Toronto London Auckland Sydney
Mexico City New Delhi Hong Kong
Danbury, Connecticut

A sea otter in the Pacific

Reading Consultant
Nanci R. Vargus, Ed.D.
Primary Multiage Teacher
Decatur Township Schools,
Indianapolis, IN

The photograph on the cover shows an underwater view of a Pacific coral reef. The photograph on the title page shows a wave in the Pacific.

Visit Children's Press® on the
Internet at:
http://publishing.grolier.com

Library of Congress Cataloging-in-Publication Data

Petersen, David, 1946-
  The Pacific Ocean / by David Petersen and Christine Petersen.
    p.   cm. — (A True book)
  Includes bibliographical references and index.
  ISBN 0-516-22043-8 (lib. bdg.)   0-516-27322-1 (pbk.)
  1. Oceanography—Pacific Ocean—Juvenile literature. 2. Pacific
Ocean—Juvenile literature. [1. Pacific Ocean. 2. Oceanography.]
I. Petersen, Christine. II. Title. III. Series.
  GC771.P47   2001
  551.46'5—dc21   00-031470

GROLIER
PUBLISHING

Contents

Pacific coastline, Oregon

Earth's Greatest Ocean

The word "ocean" comes from the ancient Greek word *Okeanos*, the name of a river that was thought to encircle the globe.

Today we know that one continuous body of water does indeed circle the Earth. It's not a river, however, but an ocean.

Often called the World Ocean,
this endless salty sea covers more
than 70 percent of Earth's surface. On maps, the World Ocean
is divided into four smaller
oceans: the Arctic, the Atlantic,
the Indian, and the Pacific.

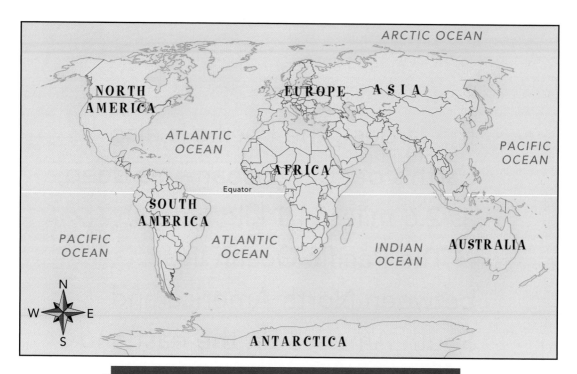

Of these four, the Pacific is the largest, painting a third of our planet a beautiful watery blue. The Pacific is so big, in fact, that the other three oceans could fit inside it. In addition to being the largest, the Pacific is also Earth's deepest ocean—as deep as 2.6 miles (4.1 kilometers).

The Pacific Ocean lies between North America and South America on the east and between Asia and Australia on the west. The northern tip of the Pacific is the Bering Strait. This narrow sea channel—only 51 mi. (82 km) wide—separates Siberia in Asia from Alaska in North America. The Bering Strait also connects the Pacific

The Bering Strait

and Arctic oceans. Far to the south, near the continent of Antarctica, the Pacific joins the Atlantic and Indian oceans.

The Pacific is dotted with thousands of islands.

At its widest—between Colombia in South America and Indonesia in Asia—the Pacific is 12,300 mi. (19,803 km) across. That's eight times as wide as the United States! Between the Pacific's far-flung shores rise more than 25,000 islands.

The "Peaceful Sea"

Ferdinand Magellan's ship *Victoria*

In the 1520s, Portuguese explorer Ferdinand Magellan became the first European to sail across the Pacific. Because he had good weather during his long voyage, Magellan named this "new" ocean *Mare Pacifico*, meaning "Peaceful Sea."

But the Pacific is not always peaceful. Powerful storms called typhoons often hit islands, coastal cities, and ships at sea.

The floor of the Pacific Ocean is also restless, often rocked by volcanic eruptions. These eruptions—like giant underwater explosions—can cause huge earthquakes.

A typhoon in Tahiti (top) and an underwater volcanic eruption near the Solomon Islands (bottom)

The Hidden Ocean Floor

Beaches don't stop where oceans begin. Underwater beaches extend hundreds of miles out to sea, forming an area called the continental shelf.

The gently slanting continental shelf ends at a depth of about 600 ft. (183 m). There the continental slope begins, diving

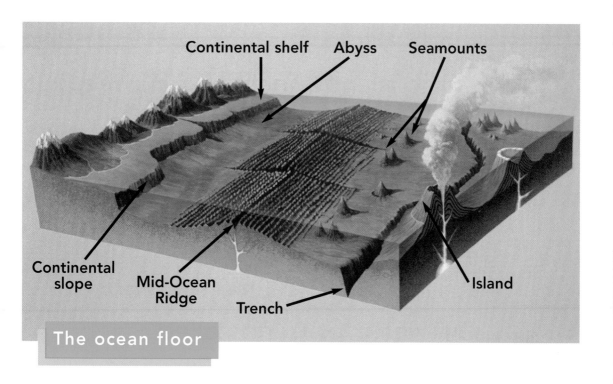

Continental shelf   Abyss   Seamounts

Continental slope

Mid-Ocean Ridge

Trench

Island

The ocean floor

steeply to the ocean floor, or abyss. The average depth of the Pacific Ocean is 13,740 ft. (4,188 m).

Underwater mountains, called seamounts, dot the Pacific ocean floor. Most

Pacific islands, including Hawaii, are the exposed tops of such seamounts. Mount Everest, in Asia, is Earth's highest mountain, rising 29,035 ft. (8,850 m) above sea level. One seamount, a Hawaiian volcano called Mauna Loa, is much taller, rising 36,201 ft. (11,034 m) above the Pacific ocean floor.

Trenches are canyons in the ocean floor. The world's deepest such canyon, near the island of Guam, is the Mariana Trench. The deepest part of the

Mauna Loa (left) and the Mariana Trench (below)

Mariana Trench

Mariana Trench, called the "Challenger Deep," lies 36,198 ft. (11,035 m) beneath the ocean surface.

Moving Waters

As sleepy as they sometimes seem, oceans are always moving. Waves form when wind blows across an ocean's surface. Waves can travel hundreds of miles before crashing against a continental shore.

Waves crashing along the Pacific coast

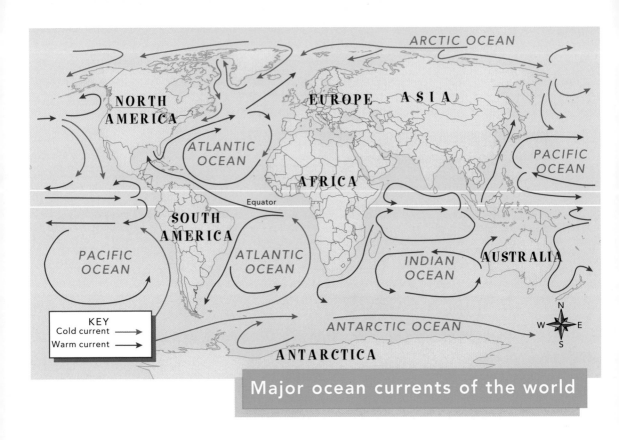

Major ocean currents of the world

Ocean currents—areas in the ocean where water moves in a certain direction—are caused by gravity and wind. Some ocean currents are like underwater rivers.

They influence the weather along their course and create "highways" for ships.

Tides, the rise and fall of Earth's oceans, are caused by the moon. On the side of Earth that faces the moon, the moon's gravitational pull causes the oceans to "bulge up" and draw away from shore, creating low tide. On the opposite side of the spinning Earth, the water also bulges outward, creating low tide there as well.

Low tide (above) and high tide (right) at a beach in California

As Earth rotates, these two high-water bulges move around the planet. In between these areas, the moon's pull is weaker. Here the oceans "flatten out" and water moves onto shore, causing high tide.

Rockin' Rollin' Waves

A tsunami hitting a town on the island of Oahu, Hawaii

Volcanoes, earthquakes, and typhoons sometimes "shake" the Pacific hard enough to create giant tidal waves. These tidal waves are called *tsunamis,* the Japanese word for "harbor waves." Tidal waves race across the ocean as fast as a jet plane— up to 500 mi. (805 km) per hour—causing great destruction. The largest tsunami on record was as tall as a 21-story building—about 210 ft. (64 m).

Kelp Beds— Floating Forests

The Pacific coast of California is home to one of Earth's greatest forests. Instead of trees, this underwater forest is filled with giant seaweed called kelp.

Kelp grows as tall as 125 ft. (38 m). Balloonlike air bladders

Underwater view of a kelp forest

Balloonlike air bladders (above) help the tops of kelp plants float on the surface of the water (right). Holdfasts (below) anchor the kelp to the ocean floor.

on the tops of each frond, or leaf, serve as floats, holding the kelp plant upright. Strong roots, called holdfasts, grip rocks on the ocean floor, anchoring the plant in place.

Kelp forests provide food and shelter for a variety of sea creatures. Starfish creep along the bottom, among the trunks of kelp. Orange fish called garibaldi find food and protection among the kelp. Sharks hunt at the edges of

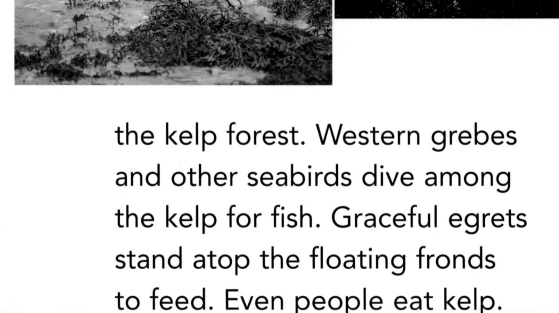

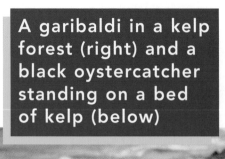

A garibaldi in a kelp forest (right) and a black oystercatcher standing on a bed of kelp (below)

the kelp forest. Western grebes and other seabirds dive among the kelp for fish. Graceful egrets stand atop the floating fronds to feed. Even people eat kelp.

Sea Otters

An otter opening a shell by beating it against a rock

Among the most lovable residents of Pacific kelp forests are sea otters. Otters are members of the weasel family. They have thick, soft fur that keeps them warm in cold water. Otters can hold their breath for up to 5 minutes as they dive for clams, sea urchins, scallops, jellyfish, crabs, and other tasty meals.

An otter opens the hard shells of its prey by floating on its back, balancing a rock on its tummy, and beating the shell against the rock until it cracks!

Living Reefs

Coral reefs form in warm, shallow water throughout the Pacific. Reefs are underwater "cities"—home to many kinds of sea animals.

In fact, coral reefs *are* animals, called polyps. These tiny, cup-shaped creatures absorb minerals from seawater and

Coral reefs are made up of millions of coral polyps.

use them to build hard external skeletons. By "gluing" themselves together, millions and millions of coral polyps form the great colonies we call coral reefs. Long after the polyps die, their hard shells remain.

Earth's largest coral reef is Australia's Great Barrier Reef.

The Great Barrier Reef, off the coast of Australia, is Earth's largest coral reef. It measures about 45 mi. (72 km) across, and is more than 1,250 mi. (2,000 km) long. That's the distance from Chicago, Illinois, to Billings, Montana.

Coral reefs, alive with color and light, are among nature's most beautiful creations. The polyps themselves are colorless. But tiny plants called algae, living inside the coral skeletons, paint the reefs in rainbows of color.

Clownfish, parrotfish, and moray eels (from left to right) are among the many colorful animals that live among Pacific coral reefs.

By day, fish with such colorful names as "parrotfish" and "clownfish" dart among the sunlit reefs. Worms and flowery sea anemones sway and dance in gentle currents. At night, nocturnal creatures such as sea urchins, octopuses, and eels emerge from hiding to feed among the coral canyons.

Pacific Travelers

Many sea animals, such as anemones, spend their entire lives in one spot. Others make long trips, called migrations.

Every winter, gray whales give birth to their young in the warm Pacific lagoons of western Mexico. Each spring, they migrate north to feed in the

Gray whales in the Pacific Ocean near Mexico

cold Pacific off the coasts of Canada and Alaska.

The moment baby sea turtles hatch—from eggs laid in beach sand—they scramble for the ocean, where they spend the rest of their lives. As adults, female sea turtles return briefly

A sea turtle laying her eggs (left) and sea turtle hatchlings making their way to the sea (above)

to their home beaches to lay their eggs—then crawl back to sea again.

The albatross has the longest wings of any bird. Its wings measure up to 11 ft. (3.4 m) from tip to tip.

Albatrosses spend most of their lives flying over the ocean.

Albatrosses spend most of their lives soaring low over the ocean, hunting fish. At night, they sleep floating on the water. Only once a year do these tireless migrators come to shore, and then just long enough to nest and raise their young.

Some humans, too, are migrators. For more than 3,000 years, Pacific island natives, known today as Polynesians, have sailed the open ocean in search of adventure and new homes. Long before Europeans first explored the Pacific, Polynesians had settled hundreds of islands there, from Midway to New Zealand and from Hawaii to Easter Island.

These early sailors traveled in giant canoes carved from

Native New Zealanders in traditional canoes in the early 1800s

trees. The biggest Polynesian canoes were 100 ft. (30.5 m) long. Their sails were woven from the tough leaves of panadus plants. These ocean-going canoes carried entire families, plus enough water and food for a trip of many weeks.

Making Peace with the Pacific

Just as it was for the Polynesians thousands of years ago, the Pacific remains one of Earth's greatest blessings today. Over half the world's supply of fish and shellfish comes from the Pacific.

The Pacific also provides vital shipping lanes between continents.

More than half the world's supply of fish and shellfish comes from the Pacific.

People pump oil and gas from beneath the ocean floor and collect salt and minerals from the water itself. And every day, millions of people play in the Pacific Ocean and on its sunny beaches.

Surfing in the Pacific

In a very real way, Earth's oceans are generous, living beings, deserving of loving care. Yet oil, sewage, garbage, and chemicals are spilled or dumped in huge amounts into the Pacific

People cleaning up an oil spill along the Pacific coast in California

every day. They poison the water, pollute the beaches, and kill fish, birds, animals, and even people. Not even the World Ocean can stand such abuse forever. Oceans—like plants, animals, and people—can sicken and die.

We must start working together right now to protect the Pacific. Then people will still be enjoying its beauty and its gifts—and adventurers will still be exploring its unsolved mysteries—3,000 years from now.

White birds flying over kelp beds in the Pacific

To Find Out More

Here are some additional resources to help you learn more about the Pacific Ocean:

Books

Dipper, Dr. Frances. **Mysteries of the Ocean Deep**. Aladdin Books, 1996.

Johnson, Jinny. **Simon and Schuster's Children's Guide to Sea Creatures.** Simon and Schuster, 1998.

Ricciuti, Edward R. **Ocean.** Benchmark Books, 1996.

Van Cleave, Janice. **Oceans for Every Kid.** John Wiley & Sons, Inc., 1996.

Waters, John F. **Deep-Sea Vents: Living Worlds Without Sun**. Cobblehill Books, 1994.

Organizations and Online Sites

Aquatic Network
http://www. aquanet.com/

A great site with general information about oceans and close-ups on such interesting topics as sharks, ocean exploration, and conservation.

The Evergreen Project— Marine Ecosystems
http://www.mobot.org/ MBGnet/salt/

Visit this web-based education site to get all the information you need on marine ecosystems.

The Monterey Bay Aquarium
886 Cannery Row
Monterey, CA 93940
http://www.mbayaq.org

This is a great place to learn all about Pacific coastal marine life. At the aquarium's website, you can take the Habitat Path to explore coastal environments, go "into" exhibits, or dive deep into the Monterey Canyon on a virtual expedition.

Nova Online: Into the Abyss
http://www.pbs.org/wgbh/ nova/abyss/

Join a scientific expedition exploring the mysteries of the deepest part of the ocean.

Ocean Planet, the Smithsonian Institution
http://seawifs.gsfc.nasa.gov: 80/OCEAN_PLANET/HTML/ ocean_planet_ocean_science.htmlsearch_educational_materials.html

Includes lesson plans, at-home projects, and fact sheets about oceans, exploration, and marine animals.

Vancouver Aquarium Marine Science Centre
PO Box 3232, Vancouver, B.C. Canada, V6B 3XB
http://www.vanaqua.org/ index2.htm

Learn about marine life and explore underwater habitats in the North Pacific, or join "Ace on the Case" to solve a mystery about the sea.

Important Words

canyon deep valley with high, steep slopes

continent one of Earth's major land areas

continuous continuing without a break; unbroken

course the path over which something moves

encircle to form a circle around

external on the outside

far-flung spread far apart

gravity the force of attraction between two objects

lagoon shallow pool or channel connected to an ocean or sea

migration the act of a group of animals or people moving from one region to another

nocturnal active at night

orbit to circle around

Index

Meet the Authors

David Petersen spent several years living, swimming, diving, and exploring beaches along the Pacific coast. He has also visited the Pacific islands of Hawaii, Guam, Japan, Okinawa, and the Philippines. Today, David lives in the mountains of Colorado, where he writes books and magazine articles about nature.

Christine Petersen is David's daughter. She grew up on the Pacific coast in California and now lives in Minneapolis, Minnesota. Chris is a biologist and educator, with a special interest in North American bats. This is the second True Book the Petersens have written together, and it won't be the last.

Photographs ©: Art Resource, NY: 38 (Giraudon); Corbis-Bettmann: 34 (Stephen Frink), 15 bottom (Roger Ressmeyer/NASA), 11 bottom (Reuters/NewMedia Inc.), 21; Dembinsky Photo Assoc.: 35 left (Bill Curtsinger), 20 (Patti McConville), 32 left (Mark J. Thomas); H. Armstrong Roberts, Inc.: 17 (D. Carriere); Liaison Agency, Inc.: 40 (Francis Li), 10 (Michael Mc Coy/FDB), 41 (Bob Torrez); NASA: 6; Peter Arnold Inc.: 29 (Fred Bavendam), 9 (Fred Bruemmer), 15 top (Doug Cheeseman), 24 bottom (Walter H. Hodge), 2 (Thomas D. Mangelsen); Photo Researchers: 11 top (Archiv), 11 center (Frederick Ayer), 32 right (David Hall), 35 right (A. Flowers & L. Newman), 36 (Frans Lanting), 27 (Pat & Tom Leeson), 32 middle (Fred McConnaughey), 23, 24 right (Gregory Ochocki), 24 left, 26 left (Stephen P. Parker); Stone: 1 (Dave Bjorn), cover, 31 (A. Witte/C. Mahaney), 30 (Paul Chesley), 26 right (Chuck Davis), 4 (Dave Schiefelbein), 43 (Baron Wolman); Woodfin Camp & Associates: 42 (A. Ramey).
Maps by Joe Le Monnier   Illustration by Lloyd K. Townsend/National Geographic Society